Also By Claire Zoghb

Small House Breathing

Boundaries

DISPATCHES FROM EVEREST

Poems

Claire Zoghb

Fomite
Burlington, VT

Poems copyright 2017 © by Claire Zoghb

All rights reserved. No part of this book may be reproduced in any form or by any means without the prior written consent of the publisher, except in the case of brief quotations used in reviews and certain other noncommercial uses permitted by copyright law.

ISBN-13: 978-1-937677-77-0

Fomite
58 Peru Street
Burlington, VT 05401
www.fomitepress.com

ACKNOWLEDGMENTS

2007 Rita Dove Poetry Award, Finalist: "Boulder"

For my father

Contents

Alabaster. Marble.	1
Black Tulip	3
Hollowed	4
Hallowed	5
Missing	6
Fossil	9
Limestone	12
Rope	13
Darkness Blossoms	14
Boulder	16
Fall	21
Last Scene:	24
After	26

Foreword

"But from Rongli they climbed steeply out of the tropical forest into the zone of flowering rhododendrons..... To flower lovers, like Howard Bury, Mallory and Wollaston, these were perpetual delight. They were all the more appreciated because they would be almost the last sign of luxuriance and grace they would behold before they had to face the austerities and stern realities of rock and ice and snow, and the frosts of Mount Everest."
– Sir Francis Younghusband,
The Epic Of Mount Everest

English mountaineer George Leigh Mallory (born June 18, 1886) and his summit partner, Andrew "Sandy" Irvine, were last seen "going strong for the top" on June 8, 1924, less than 1,000 feet from their goal.

The 1991 Mallory and Irvine Research Expedition, organized and led by Eric Simonson, located Mallory's body on the north face of Everest at 26,760 feet, within the mountain's unforgiving death zone.

The mystery persists as to whether or not the pair stood on the summit (they would have been the first to do so)—Irvine's body has not yet been recovered, nor has the team's camera.

Alabaster. Marble.

First image in the minds
of the 1999 expedition

on sighting the body:

A Greek or Roman statue

***

Mallory's mates
might have thought

datura

recalling white trumpets
phosphorescing
in Darjeeling forest night

infinite angels
announcing.

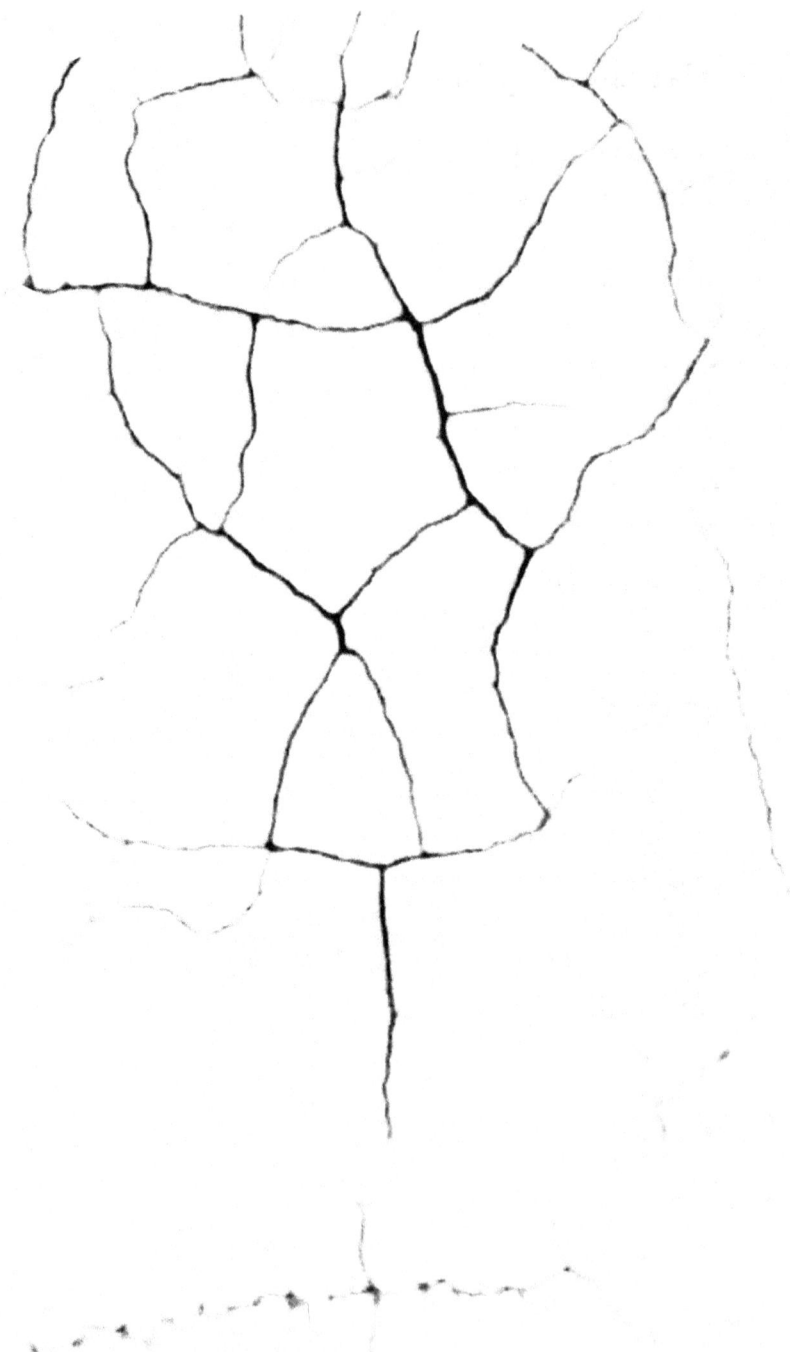

Black Tulip

What does a flower-lover do
spread out on yellow rock:

he sets down roots.

And after they cover him
with stone and prayer
and leave him
like a Persian bulb?

His face in blackness
waits to bloom.

Hollowed

Praise the jubilant beaks
        their efficient labors,
                peck by peck

Praise the blue-black eye
        its sharpness, sensing
                sustenance in scree

Praise the passionate spelunkers
        in caverns of bone,
                ruddy corporeal darkness

O liver! O lungs!
        cloud-borne
                in wheeling canopic jars!

Praise the unkindness of goraks
        their wild duty:

Praise the end of all desire.

Hallowed

Goraks feasted
but stopped short

below his heart.

What was it
that turned them
back?

Perhaps
the guardian
in each of its
chambers:

Ruth.   Clare.
Berry.   The baby.

Missing

George made this vow to Ruth:
to place her photograph
on the summit.

Doesn't every wife wish for the same?
For her black-and-white image
to be planted in ice
beside the Union Jack
five and half miles above
the living world?

The research expedition found no
photos in the tattered pockets
when they discovered his body —
frozen these seventy-five years —

face down, arms stretched
in full prostration towards the final
pyramid, bowing to that merciless
mountain who must have
simply shrugged her shoulder,
or perhaps towards Ruth,
her photograph lost longer
than Mallory ever was, clouds,
jetliners dragging shadows
across her face for decades.

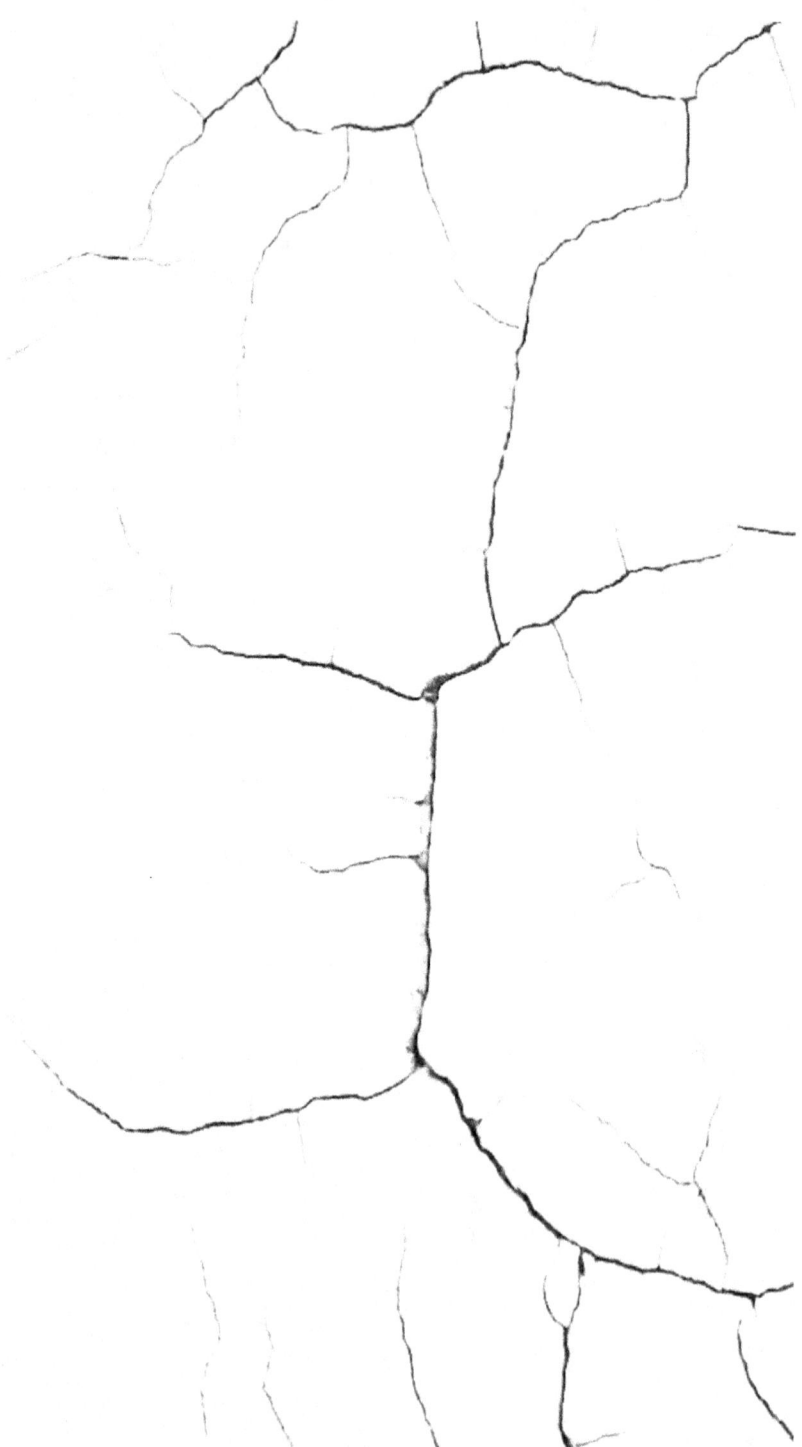

Fossil

Beached
nose-down
in scree

in Africa's
ancient scent

in salted sea gifts
deposited
here:

skeletal
fragments—

trilobites
ostracods
crinoids—

and

clenched
fists

of clamshells

ossified
before
they had
time
to open.

Limestone

layered
and familiar

as the building blocks
of his alma mater

***

its lustrous white
dressed
the range of high pyramids
rising from the Giza plateau

***

heat leaving
his luminous white skin

radiant

Rope

Praise
the umbilical—

that chunky cord

linking

life and life
light with light.

*

Pity the rope.

Once cut

birthing only
twin darknesses.

Darkness Blossoms

A sudden pressure
lands on the back of his pilot's cap,
a brief scraping of talons on leather
then a release
with a flapping of wide wings

Winds freshen
with full afternoon
then gust

the smallest of flakes
first teasing,

now furious
squalls of
white lilac and
apple blossoms
over the greenest
pastures

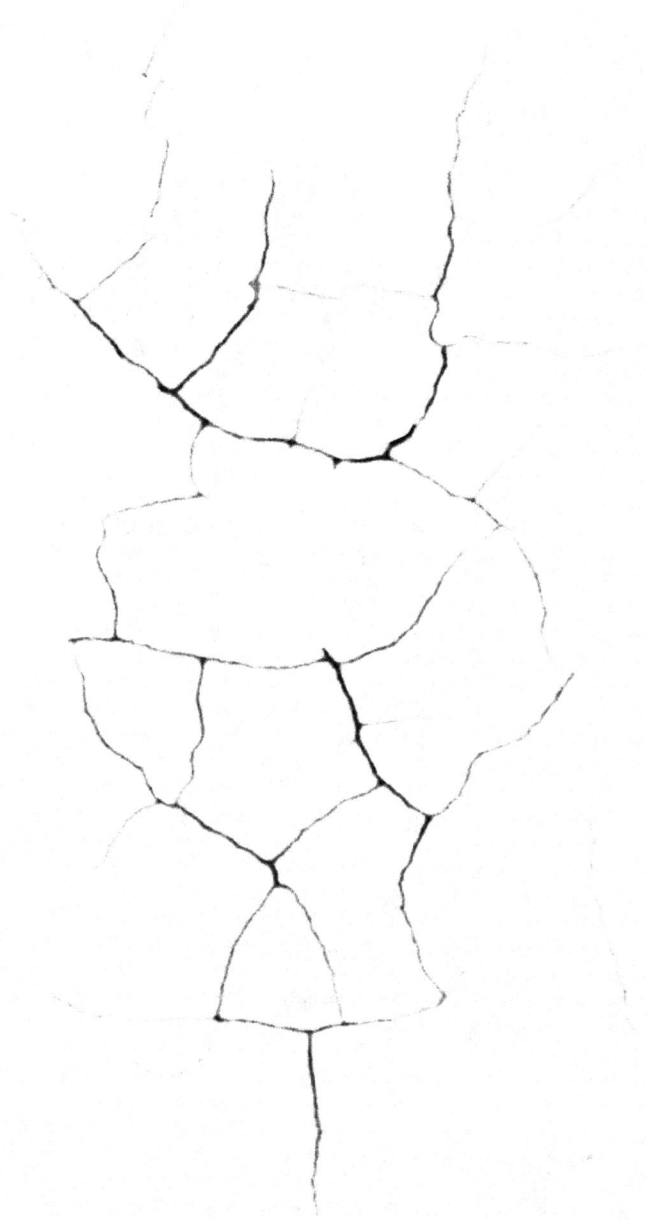

Boulder

26,760 feet

Everybody on the mountain could listen in on our radio conversations. If we found something, we didn't want some other expedition breaking the news to the world. "Boulder" was the code word for "body." – Conrad Anker

They found you, one alabaster buttock
worshipping blue-black sky.

Wool, cotton and silk
unwove their threads
in 150-mph winds,
your skin intact,
fibers holding.

When I saw the photo—
Conrad Anker hovering
over your nakedness, Yeti-sized
in his down and kevlar—I was
ashamed for you

then remembered
your penchant for skinny-dipping,
posing nude for Duncan Grant's lens (driving
those male Bloomsbury bohemians mad),
cavorting *au naturel* on neat English lawns
and stifling Asian jungles

and suddenly you looked at home,
Anker, now the alien, sliding on scree.

Missing from the photo: the hole,
gouged in your right buttock, big enough
for a gorak — the big black raven
that haunts the high Himalaya — to enter
and consume your organs one by one,
burrowing to your heart.

Only then did the mountain
give itself to you.

And from its summit,
flies a plume of snow
like a silken Buddhist scarf,
a blessing.

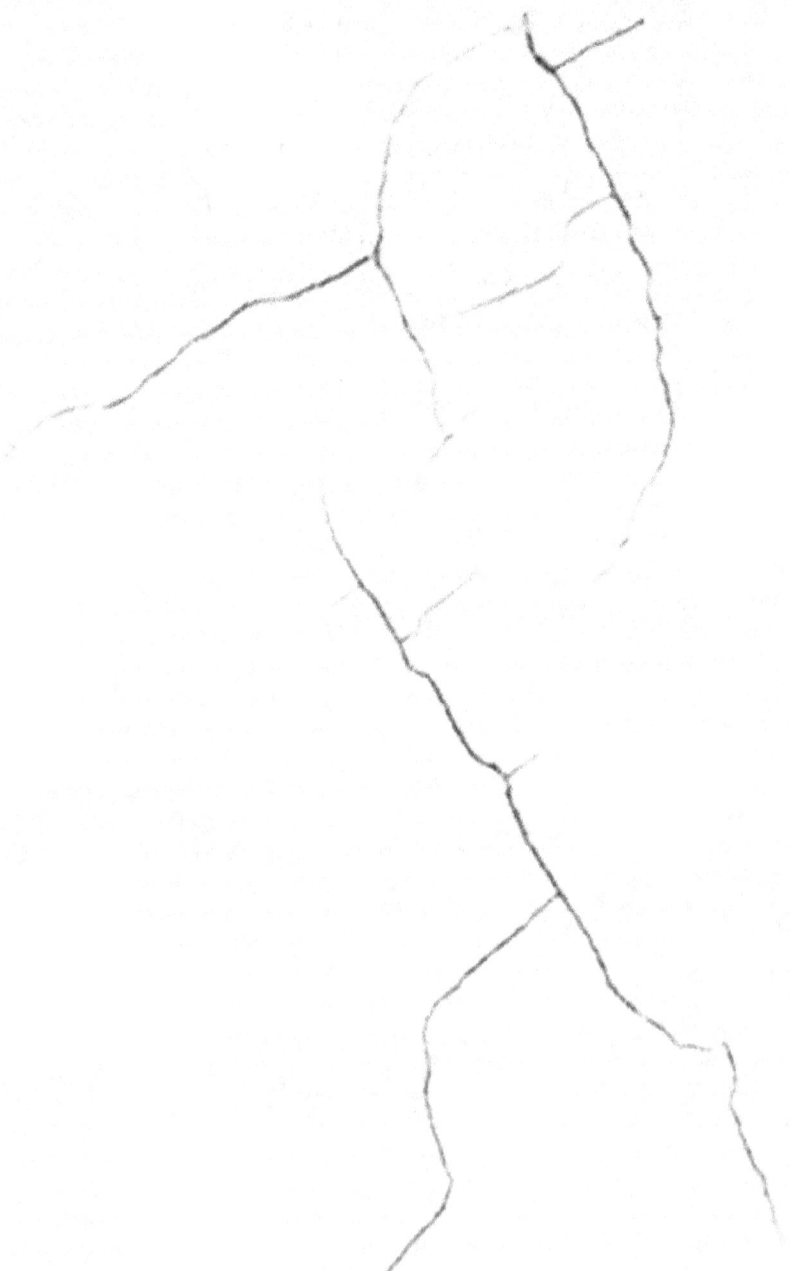

Fall

The slip—
hobnail
failure
rope
snap
ice-axe
hurtle
into
clouded
history

Crystal
beauty
icy
sharp
long
bone
breach
skin,
muffled
in
silk
linen
contained
finally
by
gabardine

Free

fall

blindness
flashes
blue-
black
sky
horizon
shift
summit
plume
smug

Ruth
Clare

slide
Berry
rock

sorry sorry
the baby
slide
crimson
burst
forehead
sliding
sliding
scree
grasp
stop

rock
bed
face
buried

visions

bottom
drops
out
of
life

only
granite
truths
now:

unyielding
mountain

yielding
breath

Last Scene:

tiny figures like
two monks on pilgrimage
in ink-washed robes
ascending a narrow ridge
going strong for the top

dark grey proceeding
through white
the way ink
edges across paper
traveling among fibers

only as far as allowed
the paper swallowing
water all the while

permitting only
palest of dried traces
to remain footprints
on the sacred
snow-covered
mountain

After

Barbarous

beautiful

the hibiscus
bursts
scarlet

blossoms
before
his eyes

before
magnolia
blooms cloud
white
the graying sky
before
his eyes

before
crabapple
blizzards
blow from
branches

before
he reaches up
with both arms
to grasp the highest apples

their skins warm
in his hands
after

NOTES

FOREWORD
Mallory and Irvine were last seen "going strong for the top" by Noel E. Odell, who was standing at 26,000 feet on the north face.

ALABASTER. MARBLE.
In Mallory's day, an attempt on Everest meant a grueling trek from the high tea-country of Darjeeling to Tibet.

FURTHER READING:

Into the Silence: The Great War, Mallory and the Conquest of Everest, by Wade Davis

Fomite

A fomite is a medium capable of transmitting infectious organisms from one individual to another.

"The activity of art is based on the capacity of people to be infected by the feelings of others." Tolstoy, What Is Art?

Writing a review on Amazon, Good Reads, Shelfari, Library Thing or other social media sites for readers will help the progress of independent publishing. To submit a review, go to the book page on any of the sites and follow the links for reviews. Books from independent presses rely on reader to reader communications.

For more information or to order any of our books, visit http://www.fomitepress.com/FOMITE/Our_Books.html

More Books from Fomite...

Joshua Amses — *Raven or Crow*
Joshua Amses — *The Moment Before an Injury*
Jaysinh Birjepatel — *The Good Muslim of Jackson Heights*
Jaysinh Birjepatel — *Nothing Beside Remains*
Antonello Borra — *Alfabestiario*
Antonello Borra — *AlphaBetaBestiaro*
Jay Boyer — *Flight*
Mike Breiner— *The Way None of This Happened*
David Brizer — *Victor Rand*
Paula Closson Buck — *Summer on the Cold War Planet*
David Cavanagh — *Cycling in Plato's Cave*
Dan Chodorkoff — *Loisada*
Michael Cocchiarale — *Still Time*
James Connolly — *Picking Up the Bodies*
Greg Delanty — *Loosestrife*
Catherine Zobal Dent — *Unfinished Stories of Girls*
Mason Drukman — *Drawing on Life*
J. C. Ellefson — *Foreign Tales of Exemplum and Woe*

Fomite

Tina Escaja — *Free Fall/Caida Libre*
Marc Estrin — *Speckled Vanities*
Zdravka Evtimova — *Carts and Other Stories*
Zdravka Evtimova — *Sinfonia Bulgarica*
Anna Faktorovich — *Improvisational Arguments*
John Michael Flynn — *Off to the Next Wherever*
Derek Furr — *Suite for Three Voices*
Derek Furr — *Semitones*
Stephen Goldberg — *Screwed and Other Plays*
Barry Goldensohn — *The Hundred Yard Dash Man*
Barry Goldensohn — *The Listener Aspires to the Condition of Music*
R. L. Green When — *You Remember Deir Yassin*
Greg Guma — *Dons of Time*
Andrei Guriuanu — *Body of Work*
Lamar Herrin — *Father Figure*
Ron Jacobs — *All the Sinners Saints*
Ron Jacobs — *Short Order Frame Up*
Ron Jacobs — *The Co-conspirator's Tale*
Zeke Jarvis — *In A Family Way*
Scott Archer Jones — *A Rising Tide of People Swept Away*
Maggie Kast — *A Free, Unsullied Land*
Darrell Kastin — *Shadowboxing With Bukowski*
Coleen Kearon — *Feminist on Fire*
Jan English Leary — *Thicker Than Blood*
Roger Lebovitz — *A Guide to the Western Slope and the Outlying Areas*
Diane Lefer — *Confessions of a Carnivore*
Marjorie Maddox — *What She Was Saying*
Kate MaGill — *Roadworthy Creature, Roadworthy Craft*
Tony Magistrale — *Entanglements*
Michele Markarian — *Unborn Children of America*
Gary Miller — *Museum of the Americas*
Ilan Mochari — *Zinsky the Obscure*
Jennifer Anne Moses — *Visiting Hours*
Sherry Olson — *Four-Way Stop*
Martin Ott — *Interrogations*

Fomite

Andy Potok — *My Father's Keeper*
Janice Miller Potter — *Meanwell*
Jack Pulaski — *Love's Labours*
Charles Rafferty — *Saturday Night at Magellan's*
Joseph D. Reich — *Connecting the Dots to Shangrila*
Joseph D. Reich — *The Hole That Runs Through Utopia*
Joseph D. Reich — *The Housing Market*
Joseph D. Reich — *The Derivation of Cowboys and Indians*
Kathryn Roberts — *Companion Plants*
Robert Rosenberg — *Isles of the Blind*
Ron Savage — *What We Do For Love*
David Schein — *My Murder and Other Local News*
Peter Schumann — *Planet Kasper, Volumes One and Two*
Peter Schumann — *Bread & Sentences*
Peter Schumann — *Faust 3*
Fred Skolnik — *Rafi's World*
Lynn Sloan — *Principles of Navigation*
L.E. Smith — *The Consequence of Gesture*
L.E. Smith — *Views Cost Extra*
L.E. Smith — *Travers' Inferno*
Robert Sommer — *A Great Fullness*
Scott T. Starbuck — *Industrial Oz*
Susan Thomas — *Among Angelic Orders*
Susan Thomas — *The Empty Notebook Interrogates Itself*
Tom Walker — *A Day in the Life*
Tom Walker — *Signed Confessions*
Sharon Webster — *Everyone Lives Here*
Susan V. Weiss —*My God, What Have We Done?*
Tony Whedon — *The Tres Riches Heures*
Tony Whedon — *The Falkland Quartet*
Peter M. Wheelwright — *As It Is On Earth*
Suzie Wizowaty —*The Return of Jason Green*
Silas Dent Zobal —*The Inconvenience of the Wings*

www.ingramcontent.com/pod-product-compliance
Lightning Source LLC
Chambersburg PA
CBHW071758080526
44588CB00013B/2295